W
What in the World?
W

Cloning: Dolly the Sheep

Teresa Wimmer

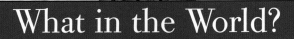

What in the World?

Creative Education
an imprint of The Creative Company

Introduction

On a quiet summer's night in July 1996, at approximately 5:00 P.M., a lamb was born in a shed amongst the green, rolling hills of a small Scottish village. She looked like any other lamb, with her curly wool coat and snow-white face—nothing anyone would have looked at twice. But this lamb was different—this lamb had no parents. Only a few staff members from the institute down the road and a veterinarian witnessed her birth. Created by a team of scientists, Dolly would change the way people everywhere viewed the miracle of life.

FICTION BONUS:
"CLONE ON THE RANGE"
BY DOUGLAS COUPLAND

TIME

Will There Ever Be Another You?

A SPECIAL REPORT ON CLONING

The March 10, 1997, issue of Time *magazine made the creation of Dolly its cover story.*

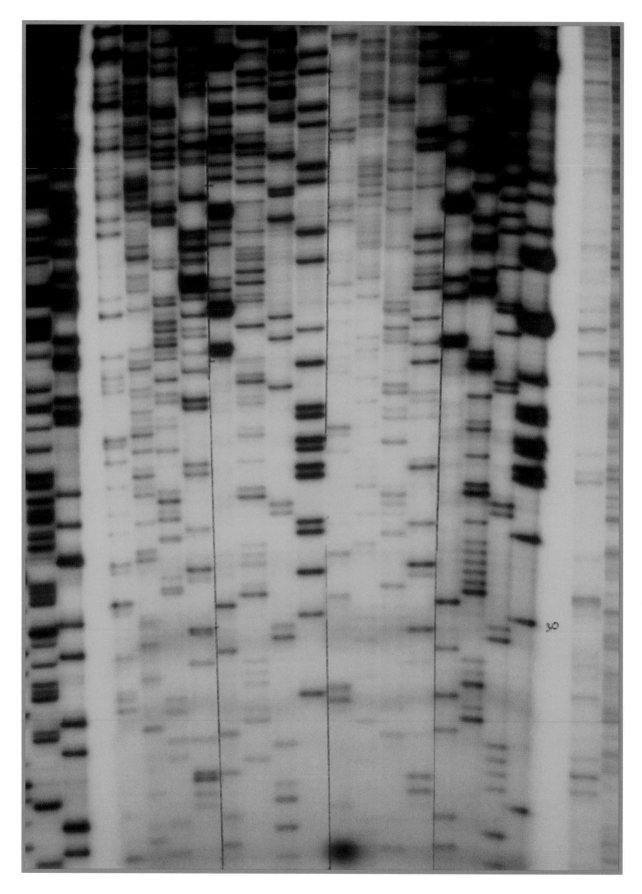

The complicated structure of a strand of DNA can be mapped and made visible as a radiograph, or image similar to an X-ray.

The sheep known as Dolly was born during a decade of many technological breakthroughs that changed the way people lived. In 1990, scientists from many countries began a project coordinated by the United States' Department of Energy and the National Institutes of Health. The purpose of

In 1990, the Hubble Space Telescope was launched into orbit around Earth. Among the thousands of images it took were some that confirmed the existence of black holes and captured a comet's collision with Jupiter.

the Human Genome Project (HGP) was to identify all 25,000 genes in the human body in order to determine what makes people's bodies the way they are. Eventually, the project's findings would enable scientists to isolate certain disease-causing genes, which would allow doctors to treat diseases more effectively.

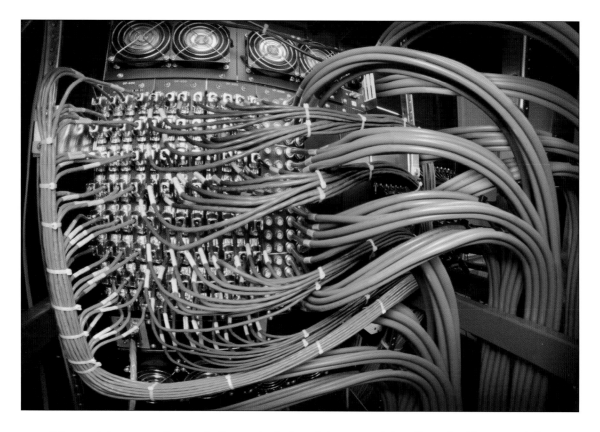

Many computer servers and communications services (such as telephone companies) use fiber optic cables to transmit data.

With the invention of the World Wide Web in the late 1980s, the 1990s became the dawn of the Information Age, and people were connected in more ways than they had ever been before. With a click of a computer mouse, people could post their own Web sites, start Web-based businesses, and retrieve information in seconds from anywhere in the world. Electronic mail, or e-mail, chat rooms, and advancements in cell phone technology also contributed greatly to the globalization of society in the 1990s.

A new age of reusable goods arrived in 1990 when the German company Wella distributed its shampoo in bottles made of Biopol, the first biodegradable plastic. Biopol is produced naturally by bacteria found in wheat.

The band Nirvana, fronted by Kurt Cobain, popularized alternative music with its 1991 album *Nevermind*. The album, which called for a rejection of commercialization in modern culture, helped start the "grunge" fashion trend.

Kurt Cobain formed his band Nirvana in 1986 and was famous for his theatrically furious performances.

Globalization meant that countries became economically interdependent as well. Relatively prosperous countries such as Australia, Ireland, Canada, the U.S., and—by the end of the decade—China that traded goods with one another enjoyed high standards of living and increased personal wealth. In contrast, when an economic recession hit Thailand in 1997, it quickly rippled throughout many Southeast Asian countries, including South Korea, Indonesia, the Philippines, and Japan, halting the decades-long progression of those countries' economies and destabilizing their currencies and stock markets.

Despite these setbacks, the global economy largely benefited from the spread of democracy and personal freedoms that took place throughout the 1990s. When the Berlin Wall, the ultimate symbol of the divisive Cold War era, was torn down in 1989, many countries began overthrowing communist governments in favor of democracy. By decade's end, reunified Germany and the former nations of the Soviet Union (which had collapsed in 1991) had grown into pro-democratic governments with more successful capitalist

The Berlin Wall, which separated East and West Berlin, was torn down in sections starting in November 1989.

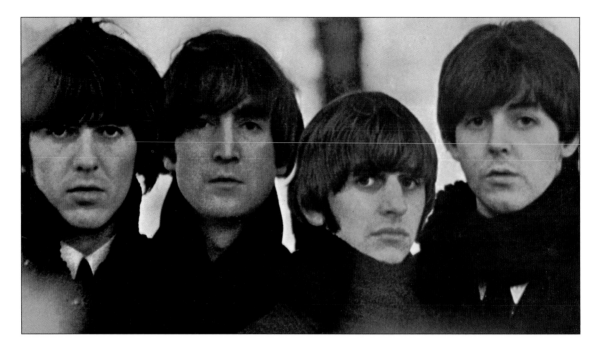

The foursome of British musicians known as the Beatles were most popular among young people of the 1960s and '70s.

economies. African countries such as Kenya, Uganda, and South Africa had also adopted democratic ideals, easing traditional media censorship in favor of the freedom of speech.

Nations with similar governments also began to share more cultural characteristics when Generation X, or people born between the mid-1960s and late 1970s, came of age during the 1990s. "Gen Xers" in the U.S. were marked by their taste for alternative rock, hip hop, and teen pop music. In Europe, Eurodance, techno, and electronica were all the rage. "Britpop" bands such as Oasis, Blur, and Pulp emerged in the mid-1990s with a new brand of British rock that set Gen Xers apart from their

In 1993, the first Beanie Babies—named Brownie and Punchers—were released in Chicago toy stores. Created by Ty, Inc., Beanies took the U.S. by storm in 1995, inspiring millions of collectors.

12

Popular outdoor music festivals such as Woodstock '94 and Woodstock '99 were held on large fields in upstate New York. Unlike the original Woodstock in 1969, these gatherings involved rioting and violence.

Harnessing the clean energy produced by giant windmills became popular during the late 1990s.

Beatles-loving parents. Teenagers all over the world felt the need to redefine both their music and their identities, which led many young people to sport tattoos and body piercings as forms of self-expression.

As countries became tied more tightly together politically, economically, and socially, they realized that they needed to work together to improve life for generations to come. When scientists and the media shed new light on the problems of global warming, a phenomenon thought to be caused by human manipulation of the environment, citizens and companies banded together

Timothy McVeigh (center, opposite) was branded as a terrorist for his instigation of the Oklahoma City bombing.

to do something about it. They were spurred to invent hybrid automobiles,
alternative fuels, and recyclable packaging, and to pass laws reducing harmful
vehicle and factory emissions.

People continued to manipulate nature, though, and scientists experimented
with genetically modified crops and injecting animals with growth hormones
to increase production yields. While many people were excited about the latest
medical or scientific breakthroughs, others began to fear how those changes
could impact their lives and the future of humankind. Then along came Dolly.

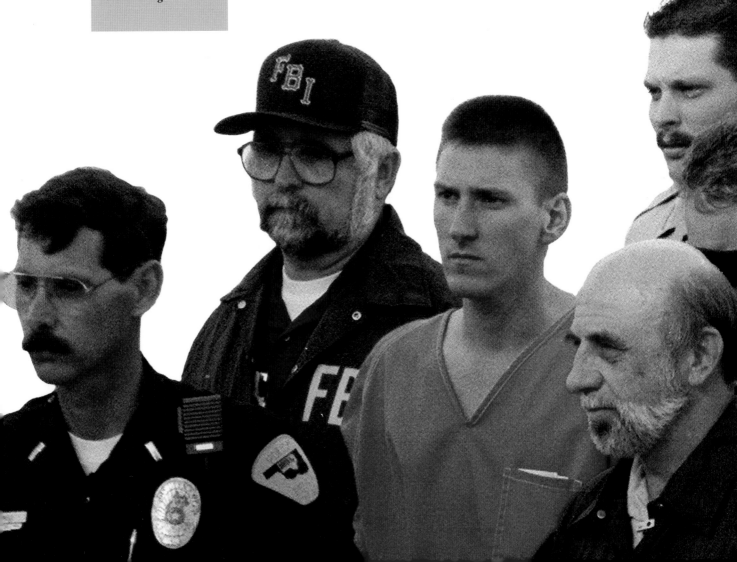

The Path to Dolly

The scientific team that produced Dolly was headed by Ian Wilmut and Keith Campbell of the Roslin Institute in Roslin, Scotland. Wilmut was born in 1944 in the rural village of Hampton Lucey, England, the son of school-teachers. As a teenager, Wilmut wanted to become a farmer, so, after high

The World Health Organization (WHO) began investigating the causes of and treatments for a world-wide obesity epidemic in 1996. The WHO classified nearly one billion adults and children as grossly overweight.

school graduation, he enrolled in England's University of Nottingham to study agriculture. While interning with the British Agricultural Research Council at Cambridge University the summer before his senior year, he discovered a deep fascination with the building blocks of life: cells.

Dr. Ian Wilmut, pictured in 1997, began working at the Roslin Institute in 1974.

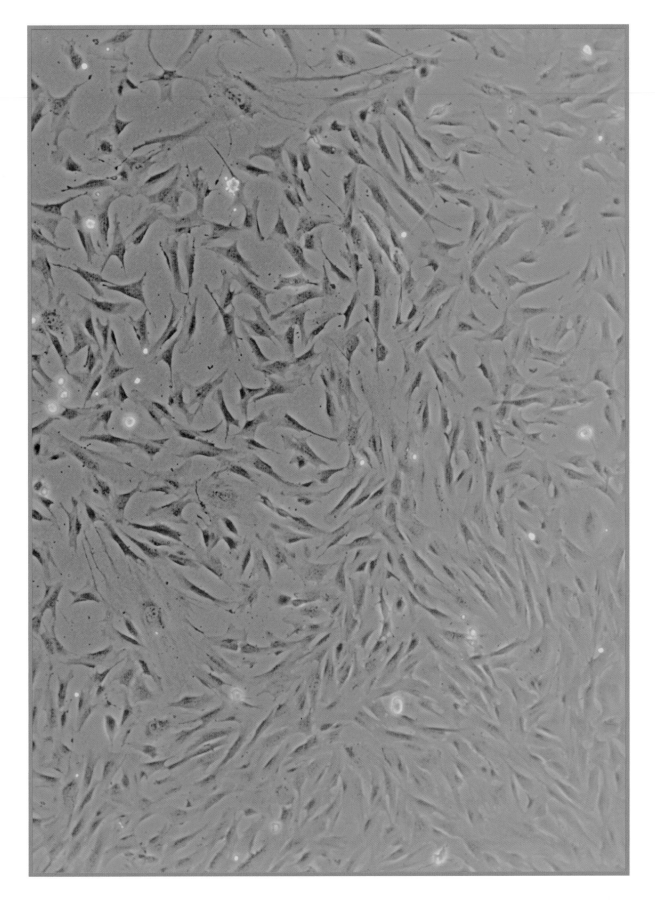

Using a microscope, people can see the tiny cells that make up every living thing, including humans and animals.

At Cambridge, Wilmut thrilled at seeing an egg from a cow or pig grow into an embryo (a group of several hundred or thousand cells) and at the possibility of altering that embryo. After receiving his undergraduate degree, Wilmut returned to Cambridge to pursue a doctoral degree in embryology. In 1973, he began work at the Animal Breeding Research Station, which later became the Roslin Institute. His work at Roslin began simply, but it soon led to an important partnership.

Keith Campbell was born in 1954 in the industrial city of Birmingham, England, and trained to be a medical technician. Soon disillusioned with that profession, Campbell returned to school. At Queen Elizabeth College in London, while studying for his bachelor's degree in microbiology, he became interested in cells and their cycles, which led him to pursue a doctoral degree at the University of Sussex in 1979. There, he worked as a research assistant, primarily researching cell growth and the cell cycles of frogs.

Hoping to colonize the moon, the Universal Lunarian Society began offering one-acre (.4 ha) sites in the lunar crater Copernicus for $50 in 1997. The colony would constitute 61 zones covered by domes containing an Earth-like atmosphere.

In 1996, Europe banned the export of British beef after British cows were found to have BSE, or "mad cow disease." Scientists found that eating tainted beef could cause the fatal Creutzfeldt-Jakob disease in humans.

Bouquets of flowers, left in memory of Princess Diana, covered the grounds of her former home at Kensington Palace (opposite).

In 1997, England's Princess Diana was killed in a car crash in Paris, France. As her many admirers around the world mourned, family members blamed the relentless hounding of the paparazzi for the accident.

Sammy Sosa, who was born in the Dominican Republic, gained fame while playing for the Chicago Cubs.

Alan Hale and Thomas Bopp discovered the Hale-Bopp comet in 1995.

Campbell became fascinated with the work Americans Robert Briggs and Thomas King had done with frogs in the 1950s. In 1952, Briggs and King had produced the world's first clones by nuclear transfer when they removed the nucleus from a frog's egg and replaced it with a new one, replacing one frog's genes with another's. From 197 reconstructed frog embryos, 27 grew into tadpoles. Campbell's interest in cloning was also piqued by the work of British scientist John Gurdon, who, in the 1960s, had conducted similar experiments, with similar success rates.

While Campbell was studying frog cells, Wilmut was at Roslin, injecting genes into undeveloped embryonic animal

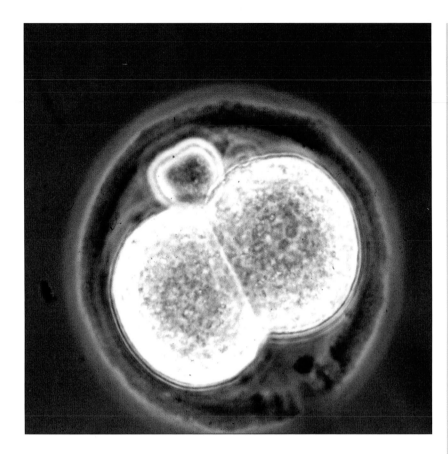

In 1998, Hawaiian researchers followed the Scottish scientists' lead and cloned a mouse.

cells to alter the makeup of the embryo. Wilmut knew the growth cycle well. As life is forming, each cell grows from a blank, embryonic cell into a specialized cell—it changes form and takes on the function of a skin, bone, muscle, or tissue cell. Wilmut thought it would be more challenging to grow older cells in the lab and add genes to them, instead of starting with younger cells that were essentially blank slates. The problem was that older cells, which had already taken on their

Because of Dolly's intense media coverage, she was not as shy around humans as sheep usually are. She often ran to the front of her pen to greet visitors, especially if they had brought treats.

final form, could not be added to embryos without modification. But, inspired by the work of Danish scientist Steen Willadsen, who had used embryonic cells to clone a lamb in 1984, Wilmut dedicated his future work to achieving what had long seemed impossible—cloning a mammal from an adult cell. The only way to do that would be to clone adult cells after the genes had been removed. That complicated procedure had never been done before. Wilmut needed help.

In 1990, Campbell was implanting human DNA into frog cells at Scotland's University of Dundee. He found that, once the DNA was inside the cell, the frog cell modified the structure of the human DNA to look like a frog nucleus. This finding convinced Campbell that it was possible to trick an egg cell into using a foreign nucleus, and that embryonic, unspecialized cells were not needed

Dolly (middle) looked just like any other Finn Dorset sheep, but she was inherently different.

An admirer of sheep, English sculptor Henry Moore designed a bronze work for the animals in a neighboring field.

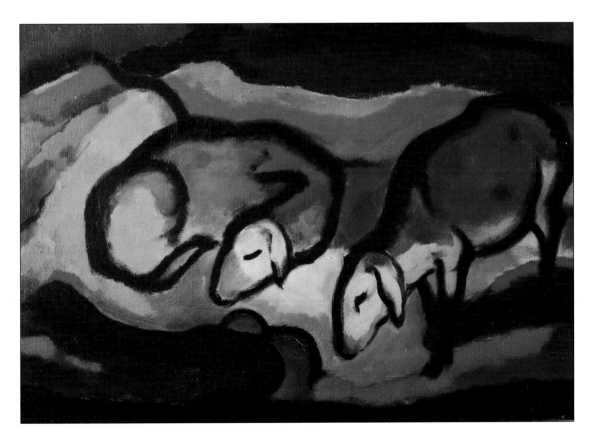

Another modernist artist, German Franz Marc, was known for his mystical paintings of animals such as Sheep, 1912.

Morag (above) and Megan (opposite) served as the precursors to Dolly and represented a breakthrough in cloning.

to clone a mammal. A year later, he brought his findings to the Roslin Institute and, because of his expertise in cell cycles, was tasked to work with Wilmut.

After four years of genetic experimentation, Wilmut and Campbell finally succeeded in cloning mammals. In 1995, two sheep named Megan and Morag were cloned from cells taken from nine-day-old embryos. These cells were notable because they were cultured (grown in a dish in the lab) after removal from the original organism and had already changed form to become specialized skin cells in the culture. For the first time, two live, healthy lambs were born from cells that had been cloned from specialized cells. Wilmut and Campbell couldn't help but wonder if they could clone a mammal from even older, more specialized cells—from adult cells.

Hello, Dolly

Even though the births of Megan and Morag were a significant step in the cloning of mammals, few scientists around the world took notice. Because the work was done at a rural research center and not at a university, and on farm animals instead of laboratory mice, it barely made news. Nevertheless, Wilmut and

Ian Wilmut's father suffered from a severe case of diabetes that caused blindness for the last 30 years of his life. The desire to prevent this disease was partly why Wilmut became interested in genetic engineering.

Campbell were curious about the next step—they wanted to see how far they could push the boundaries of cloning and the limits of their imaginations.

With funds from a small chemical company named PPL Therapeutics, Wilmut and Campbell began a new project in 1996. PPL provided frozen

Dolly (opposite and above) was a triumph for Dr. Ian Wilmut (above) and his team.

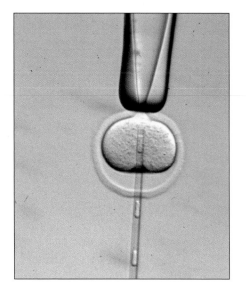

mammary cells from a six-year-old Finn Dorset ewe, a sheep breed characterized by its gray fleece and snow-white face. Wilmut and Campbell put the mammary cells in a culture dish in the lab so that they could manipulate the cells back into an unspecialized state. Then they took 430 eggs from Scottish Blackface sheep and removed the nuclei, the parts of the cells that store genetic material. The empty eggs were electrically shocked so that the genetic material of the adult cells, which had also been shocked to break through the cells' DNA proteins, would ooze into the eggs. The electric current tricked the modified eggs into believing they had been newly fertilized, making them ready to produce new life. Out of 270 successfully fused eggs, Wilmut and Campbell got 29 embryos. They then transferred the embryos into the wombs of 13 surrogate sheep mothers.

The Scottish Blackface surrogates were closely monitored. After 110 days had passed, the scientists did ultrasounds on all the sheep and found that all but one of the fetuses had been lost, apparently miscarried. But the sheep that carried that lone surviving fetus gave birth on July 5, 1996, and out came Dolly. She weighed 14.5 pounds (6.6 kg) and looked nothing like the Blackface sheep that had given birth to her. With her white face and light gray fleece, Dolly looked like a copy of the original Finn Dorset ewe.

Scientists use instruments called micropipettes to inject the nucleus of a cell and remove its genetic information.

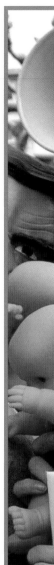

From the start, Ian Wilmut's experiments with cloning mammals were controversial. In 1991, a group of animal activists burned down a portion of his laboratory in protest. He rebuilt and continued his work.

Groups opposed to Wilmut's advances in cloning research begged him to not touch humans, displaying signs to that effect.

Archaeologists have found evidence that people kept sheep as long as 11,000 years ago. Prehistoric sheep were tall, brown, and hairy. Through the years, sheep have become whiter and woollier, with smaller eyes and brains.

The birth of Dolly, whom Wilmut named after American country and western singer Dolly Parton, was a momentous occasion. Wilmut and Campbell kept her birth a secret while they genetically tested her DNA to determine if she was, in fact, a clone. It was true—Dolly's DNA was identical to that of the original Finn Dorset. In February 1997, Wilmut and Campbell officially announced her birth, and this time, the world took notice.

In the weeks and months after Dolly's birth, thousands of journalists from all over the world descended on the tiny village of Roslin. They demanded to see Dolly

Singer and actress Dolly Parton provided a famous name for the cloned sheep.

Many wild mountain sheep do not live beyond age six or seven. Their teeth wear away from the winters spent chewing rock-hard turnips. Once their teeth are gone, they can no longer eat and therefore die.

Scottish sheep must be highly adaptable to the rugged land and harsh climate found in the high country of Scotland.

In 2005, Wilmut and his colleagues were given permission to clone human embryos for research purposes.

Dolly was an instantaneous celebrity, commanding the attention of major news organizations around the world.

The fat from sheep, known as tallow, is used to make candles and soap. The tallow is cooked to be purified, and then it is molded into candles or bars of soap.

and insisted on interviewing Wilmut and Campbell, who were bombarded with phone calls, e-mail messages, and requests for interviews and speaking engagements. Once, this prompted the Roslin scientists to declare a "media-free day," in which they locked themselves in their lab and hid Dolly.

Throughout her life, Dolly would be the object of much scrutiny. She was usually kept in her pen at Roslin and not allowed to roam outside with the other sheep for security reasons. She looked like any other Finn Dorset sheep, but Wilmut and Campbell wanted to see if she functioned like other sheep,

A lamb drinks its

mother's milk for about

four months and then

moves on to eating

hay, grass, and grain.

Lambs can walk within

minutes of birth.

The sheep in Edmond Tschaggeny's 1867 painting Shepherdess Resting with Her Flock *(above) feature naturally long tails.*

so they bred her with a Welsh Mountain ram named David. In 1998, Dolly gave birth to a lamb named Bonnie, and, one year later, to triplets. All were born healthy.

Dolly's birth sparked questions about the possibility, benefits, drawbacks, and ethical responsibility of cloning humans. Government officials, scientists, and the general public joined in the debates. Those who saw the positive potential argued that cloning humans would make organ transplants more successful, as the new organ could come from the person's own genetic twin.

Sheep are born with long tails. Shortly after birth, the tails are shortened to keep them free of dirt and manure. In some parts of the world, though, the tails are left long.

Genetics programs at American universities sometimes received funding from the state to work on stem cell research.

Those who disagreed with the practice pointed to the unpredictability of cloning animals, which often resulted in animals being susceptible to early disease or malfunctioning organs, and feared similar results if humans were cloned.

Although many worried that cloning humans would mean a loss of respect for human life, people were awestruck at the Roslin scientists' achievement, recognizing that the world had entered a new genetic age. Nearly every week, news reports carried scientists' discoveries of the latest gene linked to disease or behavior patterns. As the study of genetics advanced, some people

In 2000, a Japanese couple had their wedding photo taken with Dolly. Fearing others would follow suit and bombard Dolly with further attention, researchers put a stop to the practice.

In the 1990s, American artist Chuck Close was best known for his technique of creating portraits using colorful tiles placed in a grid and painted with abstract shapes. Such work was showcased at New York City's Museum of Modern Art in 1998.

In 2005, the Human
Fertilization and
Embryology Authority
allowed Ian Wilmut
to clone human
embryos in order to
find the cause of the
motor neuron disease
Amyotrophic Lateral
Sclerosis (ALS, or Lou
Gehrig's Disease).

envisioned—and feared—a world of human sheep devoid of the ability to form independent opinions. Both Wilmut and Campbell spoke out publicly against human cloning.

When Dolly developed arthritis in 2002, some scientists wondered whether her aging had been accelerated, since she had started life at the halfway point—most sheep live to age 10 or 12, and Dolly had been cloned from a 6-year-old. Although Dolly eventually died of lung disease on February 14, 2003, her impact on the field of genetic engineering continues to be seen.

Famous scientist Stephen Hawking (opposite) suffers from ALS; Dolly's first fleece was knitted into a sweater.

Scientists in Seoul, South Korea, created the first cloned dog, an Afghan hound named Snuppy (above, right), in 2005.

Since Dolly's birth, scientists have successfully cloned mice, pigs, horses, cats, and dogs, many of which had been thought too complex to clone. By cloning animals from adult cells, scientists are better able to understand how to treat diseases, prolong health, and preserve life, both in animals and humans. That knowledge, perhaps, is Dolly's greatest achievement.

Because of Dolly, no longer will people think of sheep simply as the herd animals so often portrayed in paintings (opposite).

What in the World?

1944	Ian Wilmut is born in Hampton Lucey, England.
1945	The U.S.'s use of atomic bombs in Japan leads to the swift end of World War II.
1948	The country of Israel is founded to provide a haven for Jewish refugees from war-torn Europe.
1951	The first successful cattle embryo transplants are performed at the University of Wisconsin-Madison.
1954	Keith Campbell is born in Birmingham, England.
1955	The Disneyland theme park opens in Anaheim, California.
1962	American author Rachel Carson publishes *Silent Spring*, which highlights worldwide environmental problems caused by humans.
1967	The first Super Bowl, between the Green Bay Packers and the Kansas City Chiefs, is played.
1971	Floppy disks for computers are introduced as a convenient way to store and transport computer data.
1975	Communist dictator Pol Pot begins his reign of terror in Cambodia, killing 2 million people.
1978	The world's first test-tube baby, Louise Joy Brown, is born in Great Britain.
1984	Chinese scientists successfully clone a fish, a golden carp.
1990	The Human Genome Project is established to decipher the human genetic code.
1994	The Channel Tunnel opens, connecting Great Britain and France via the world's longest undersea tunnel.
1996	Dolly is born at the Roslin Institute in Roslin, Scotland.
2001	Terrorist planes crash into the World Trade Center towers in New York City, killing thousands.
2003	Dolly dies from a progressive lung disease at the Roslin Institute.

Copyright

Published by Creative Education
P.O. Box 227, Mankato, Minnesota 56002

Creative Education is an imprint of The Creative Company.
Design by Rita Marshall
Production design by The Design Lab

Photographs by Alamy (Epicscotland.com, Nic Cleave Photography, PHOTOTAKE Inc.), Art Resource (Giraudon, Nicolas Sapieha), Associated Press, Corbis (Najlah Feanny/CORBIS SABA, MCPHERSON/COLIN/ CORBIS SYGMA), Getty Images (Charles James Adams, AFP PHOTO/ FILES/ALESSANDRO ABBONIZIO/COLIN MCPHERSON, MAR-TIN BERNETTI/AFP, Rosa Bonheur, Tim Boyle, JIM COLBURN/AFP, Matt Cardy, James Crump/WireImage, BOB DAEMMERICH/AFP, Deutsche Bundesbank, Peter Essick/Aurora, Stephen Ferry/Liaison, Jayne Fincher, Christopher Furlong, Tim Graham, Paul Harris, HENNING KAI-SER/AFP, Lester Lefkowitz, GERARD MALIE/AFP, Brad Mangin/MLB Photos, Dan McCoy–Rainbow, Michael Ochs Archives, MPI, JOYCE NALTCHAYAN/AFP, MARTIN OESER/AFP, Matthew Pace, Seoul National University, GEORGE SHELTON/AFP, MIKE SIMMONDS/ AFP, Time Inc./Time Life Pictures, Edmond Jean-Baptiste Tschaggeny, Cornelis van Leemputten), iStockphoto (Molnár Ákos, Eric Isselée)

Photograph copyright © 2008 Marcel Imsand (1, 32–33)

Library of Congress Cataloging-in-Publication Data
Wimmer, Teresa.
Cloning: Dolly the sheep / by Teresa Wimmer.
p. cm. — (What in the world?)
Includes index.
ISBN 978-1-58341-652-5
1. Cloning—Juvenile literature. 2. Dolly (sheep)—Juvenile literature. I. Title. II. Series.

QH442.2W55 2008   660.6'5—dc22   2007006946

First Edition
9 8 7 6 5 4 3 2 1

Index